Was ... *.C.*

Washington, D.C.

c2

Albany, NY 12208

Albany, NY 12208

Steck-Vaughn Company

Executive Editor	Diane Sharpe
Senior Editor	Martin S. Saiewitz
Design Manager	Pamela Heaney
Photo Editor	Margie Foster

Proof Positive/Farrowlyne Associates, Inc.
Program Editorial, Revision Development, Design, and Production

Consultant: E. Missy Daniels, Special Projects Manager, Office of Tourism and Promotions

Published by Raintree Steck-Vaughn Publishers, an imprint of Steck-Vaughn Company.

A Turner Educational Services, Inc. book. Based on the Portrait of America television series by R. E. (Ted) Turner.

Cover Photo: Lincoln Memorial by © Chuck Peflley / Tony Stone Images

Library of Congress Cataloging-in-Publication Data

Thompson, Kathleen.
    Washington, D.C. / Kathleen Thompson.
        p.   cm. — (Portrait of America)
    "A Turner book."
    "Based on the Portrait of America television series"—T.p. verso.
    Includes index.
    ISBN 0-8114-7394-5 (library binding).—ISBN 0-8114-7475-5 (softcover)
    1. Washington (D.C.)—Juvenile literature. [1. Washington (D.C.)]
I. Title. II. Series: Thompson, Kathleen. Portrait of America.
F194.3.T47 1996
975.3—dc20
                                      95-40013
                                      CIP
                                      AC

Printed and Bound in the United States of America

2 3 4 5 6 7 8 9 10 WZ 03 02 01 00 99

Acknowledgments
The publishers wish to thank the following for permission to reproduce photographs:
Pp. 7, 8 © Photri; p. 10 Maryland Historical Society; p. 11 (both) Architect of the Capitol; p. 12 From the American Geographical Society Collection, University of Wisconsin-Milwaukee Library; p. 13 Historical Society of Washington, D.C.; p. 14 Maryland Historical Society; pp. 15, 16, 17 © Michael Reagan; p. 18 (top) National Portrait Gallery, Smithsonian Institution, (bottom) AP/Wide World; p. 19 (top) District of Columbia Public Library, (bottom) Congress of the United States, House of Representatives; pp. 20, 22, 23 The Bettmann Archive; p. 24 Smithsonian Institution, National Portrait Gallery; p. 25 Maryland Historical Society; p. 26 © Photri; p. 28 © Michael Reagan; p. 29 (top) © Brad Markel/Gamma-Liaison, (bottom) White House Photos; p. 30 U.S. Department of the Treasury; p. 31 (top) © Wesley Hitt/Gamma-Liaison, (bottom) © Gerard Rancinan/Gamma-Liaison; p. 32 Keith Jewel/U.S. Capitol Office of Photography; p. 34 © Uniphoto; p. 36 National Museum of African Art, Smithsonian Institution; p. 37 (top) National Gallery of Art, Smithsonian Institution, (right) Architect of the Capitol; p. 38 (top left) © Michael Reagan, (top right) Lee Stalsworth/Hishorn Museum/Smithsonian Institution; 39 (top) © Carol Pratt/John F. Kennedy Center for the Performing Arts, (center right) Jessie Cohen/National Zoological Park/Smithsonian Institution, (bottom) © Eric Futran/Gamma-Liaison; pp. 40, 41 Washington National Cathedral; p. 42 © Mark Reinstein/Uniphoto; p. 44 © Michael Reagan; p. 47 (left) © Vireo, (right) © Photo Researchers.

STECK-VAUGHN

PORTRAIT OF AMERICA

Washington, D.C.

Kathleen Thompson

A Turner Book

RSVP

RAINTREE
STECK-VAUGHN
PUBLISHERS

The Steck-Vaughn Company

Austin, Texas

Washington, D.C.

Potomac River

WASHINGTON, D.C.

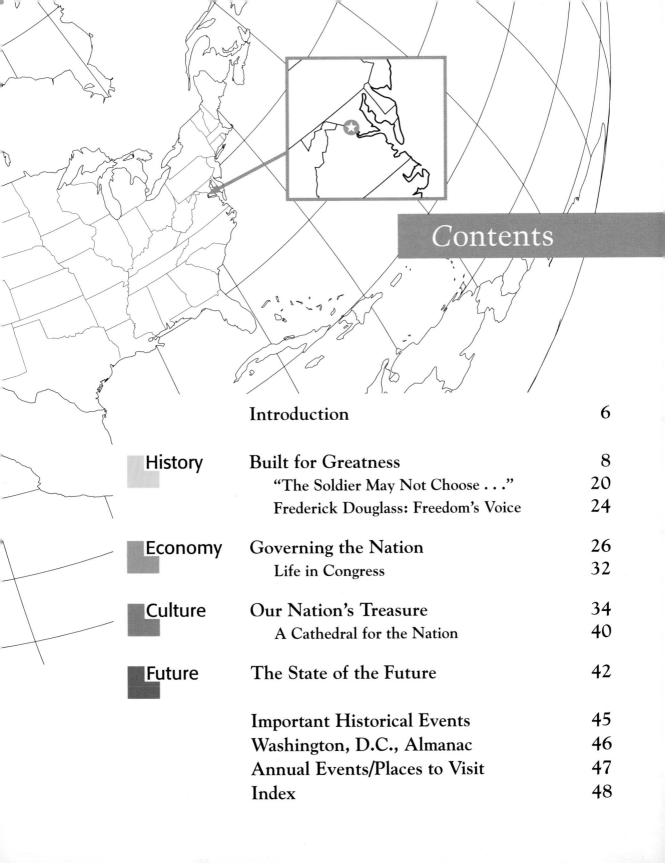

Contents

Introduction

You have no doubt heard of the White House, the Lincoln Memorial, and the Washington Monument. They are world-famous landmarks located in Washington, D.C. This bustling area didn't begin as a fort or trading post. It didn't spring up naturally at a place where two roads crossed. The District of Columbia was made to order. It was specially created for just one reason: to serve as the nation's capital. The business of Washington, D.C., is government. It's a place all its own—rich in history and making more history every day.

The Georgetown University crew team rows on the Potomac River. The Potomac forms part of the border between Washington, D.C., and Virginia.

Washington, D.C.

Built for Greatness

Hundreds of years ago, a group of Algonquin called the Piscataway lived along the Potomac and Anacostia rivers. They grew their own vegetables in nearby fields. They protected their villages with palisades, high fences made of wooden logs set upright.

Native Americans had lived in this area for a long time. The Piscataway and other Algonquin used soapstone to make arrowheads, knives, and other tools. They mined the soapstone from a nearby quarry, or pit. Archaeologists estimate that people had used the quarry for about six thousand years.

In 1608 Captain John Smith led the first group of Europeans to explore the Potomac River area. There they met Native Americans called the Nacostin. The Anacostia River is named after their village. Europeans continued to move into the region, so around 1680 the Piscataway moved west and joined groups of the Iroquois Federation. After that, the English dominated the region.

In 1792 a contest was held for the design of the United States Capitol. Although James Thornton's design won, the construction was supervised by several other architects.

Historians believe that there were two Algonquin settlements in the Washington, D.C., area, one on either side of the Potomac River. The Algonquins on the Potomac lived in wooden houses near their fields of crops.

As the British colonies grew, the Potomac River became the border between the Virginia colony and the Maryland colony. Each state had a port town on the river—George Town, in Maryland, and Alexandria, in Virginia. Tobacco plantations surrounded the ports, which were the places where plantation owners shipped out their crops. The ships sailed down the Potomac to the Atlantic Ocean.

The colonists resented Great Britain's rules and protested unfair laws. In 1775 delegates from each of the 13 colonies decided to fight for independence from Great Britain. The colonists chose George Washington to command their military. Many men were killed in battles that took place from South Carolina to New York. Finally, in 1781 the Revolutionary War ended when the British Army surrendered at Yorktown, Virginia. The 13 colonies no longer belonged to Great Britain; now they were the 13 United States of America. The states began the work of setting up a federal government. In 1787 the Constitution was completed. Two years later, George Washington was elected as the first President of the new country.

The question of where the new nation's capital would be located was debated by the nation's leaders. During the war, the Continental Congress had met in Philadelphia. After the war, the government met in several cities, including Philadelphia, Pennsylvania; Princeton and Trenton, New Jersey; New York City, New York; and Annapolis, Maryland. Northerners and southerners believed that the country's capital would become an economic center, so both sides wanted it.

There was another issue to be resolved: Who should pay the debts that the states had acquired during the war? Secretary of the Treasury Alexander Hamilton wanted the federal government to take over these bills. He felt the government should be given the right to tax certain items to pay off the bills. Secretary of State Thomas Jefferson didn't want a strong federal government, so he disagreed with Hamilton's plan. Finally, Hamilton and Jefferson worked out a compromise that also solved the problem of paying the debt.

Hamilton got his wish that the federal government would pay the states' bills, and Jefferson agreed only if the capital would be in a southern area. To ensure that no state would become much more powerful than any other, Alexander Hamilton persuaded everyone that no single state should own the land where the capital was to be built. The new District of Columbia would belong to the whole nation.

Italian artist Constantino Brumidi worked for twenty years on this painting inside the Capitol dome. The painting is called "The Apotheosis of Washington."

Originally the dome of the Capitol was made of wood and copper. That dome was replaced with a cast iron dome in the 1850s.

PLAN
of the CITY of
Washington
in the Territory of Columbia
ceded by the States of
VIRGINIA and MARYLAND
to the
United States of America
and by them established as the
SEAT of their GOVERNMENT
after the Year
MDCCC.

GEORGE TOWN

Capitol......38:53. N.
Long......... 0: 0.

OBSERVATIONS
explanatory of the
Plan.

Breadth of the Streets.

L'Enfant's map shows
the original design of
Washington, D.C.

Both Virginia and Maryland gave up property along the Potomac River for the new capital city. It was shaped like a diamond, ten miles long on each side. The city was named after George Washington, in honor of his service to the country as general and as President.

President Washington hired Pierre Charles L'Enfant to design the capital city. L'Enfant was a French architect who had fought in the Revolutionary War. He had already designed some buildings for the American government. L'Enfant worked with two other people. One was Major Andrew Ellicott, a surveyor. A surveyor is someone who measures the exact dimensions of land. Ellicott was accompanied by his assistant, Benjamin Banneker. Banneker was a free African American who was also a mathematician and an astronomer.

L'Enfant had a vision for the city. The Capitol, the actual building where the Congress would meet, would be in the center. Streets would extend out from the Capitol like the spokes in a wheel. There would be special places for parks and monuments. The work began. But L'Enfant argued continually with the Board of Commissioners. The commissioners felt that they were in charge and L'Enfant should do as he was told. L'Enfant was committed to his plan and he refused. L'Enfant was fired, but he accomplished what he had set out to do. He had designed a grand capital.

Washington, D.C., officially became the capital in 1800, and the federal government moved there from Philadelphia. The government at that time consisted of President John Adams, Vice President Thomas Jefferson, 32 senators, 106 members of Congress, and about 131 federal employees. All in all, about eight thousand people lived in the District of Columbia.

For a long time the people who lived in the city called it "Wilderness City." The streets weren't paved, and there was no running water and no sewers. Pigs and cattle roamed the city—they made enough noise to keep people awake at night.

This medal features Pierre L'Enfant.

The United States Constitution said that Congress governed the district. But in 1802 Congress created a local government that allowed the citizens of Washington, D.C., to vote for city council members.

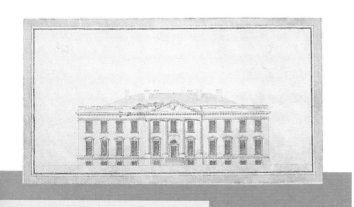

Artist James Hoban designed the original White House.

Eighteen years later the people were given the right to elect their own mayor. They were not allowed to vote for members of Congress or for President, however.

In 1812 the United States and Great Britain went to war again. The British Army advanced up the Potomac River to the capital in August 1814. President James Madison was not in the city when the British Army arrived. First Lady Dolley Madison left the capital with important government papers, Gilbert Stuart's portrait of George Washington, and other valuables. The British burned many government buildings, including the White House.

The burning of Washington, D.C., had a strong effect on the people of the United States. They developed a proud attachment to the country's capital. But Washington, D.C., did not grow as expected. The city was in debt and the living conditions were bad. So, in 1846 Congress allowed the part of the territory originally donated by Virginia to return to that state.

When the Civil War began in 1861, Washington, D.C., was in a dangerous position. To the south was Virginia, which was a Confederate state. To the north was Maryland, which had been a slave state. Although many people in Maryland sided with the Confederates, the state stayed with the Union. Washington, D.C., was the capital of the Union, so it had to be protected. At times more than fifty thousand soldiers were stationed in Washington, D.C. The Mall between the Capitol and the Washington Monument became a pasture for about thirty thousand military horses. The city's federal buildings—even the Capitol itself—became hospitals for thousands of wounded soldiers. Sanitation was poor, and diseases swept through the city.

The two main issues of the Civil War were slavery and states' rights. The northern and southern states had disagreed about which powers individual states or the federal government should have. When the Union won the Civil War, the federal government was assured its power over the states in many areas. As a result, Washington, D.C., became more important. The city's population grew. Before the Civil War, about seventy thousand people lived in Washington, D.C. After the war, its population was about one hundred thousand. More work had to be done on the city in order to make it a place worthy of a capital city and to make it a comfortable place for its citizens to live.

In 1871 President Ulysses S. Grant appointed Alexander Shepherd as head of the city's Board of Public Works. Following L'Enfant's plan, Shepherd filled in a large canal that was full of sewage. Work crews paved over eighty miles of city streets. Other streets were dirt roads, and Shepherd had workers pack them down and make them level. They planted trees and put in hundreds of miles of sidewalks and water, gas, and sewer lines.

Arlington National Cemetery is across the Potomac River, in Virginia. The cemetery honors men and women who have served in any branch of the armed forces.

The Tomb of the Unknowns was erected after World War I. The monument honors all soldiers who have died in defense of our country, especially those whom the government could not identify.

Shepherd estimated that the project would cost $6 million, but it actually cost $18 million. Half of the people on the Board of Public Works were elected by the people of the city, and they had approved Shepherd's budget for the project. Many members of Congress felt that the expense of the project showed that the citizens couldn't govern themselves very well. So Congress changed the laws. Washington, D.C., became the only city in America that was not allowed to elect its own officials. After all the changes, the city's growth slowed.

In 1901 Congress decided to build several parks. The architects in charge went back to L'Enfant's plan, which included open areas with statues, trees, and gardens. But some parts of the building project were delayed because of World War I, which the United States entered in 1917. During this time the powers of the national government greatly expanded. The city experienced another population boom. Temporary buildings were built on the Mall. City services were stretched to the limit once again.

The war ended in 1918, and the architects returned. The Lincoln Memorial was completed, and the National Gallery of Art and the Jefferson Memorial were built. At the same time, the city began to struggle with a problem that was growing everywhere in the nation. Living conditions were very bad for poor African American residents in the city. Like other southern cities, Washington, D.C., was segregated. This meant that there were separate facilities for African Americans—facilities such as restaurants, drinking fountains, movie theaters, schools, and even seating on buses. Race riots broke out in 1919. When the Lincoln Memorial was dedicated in 1922, African Americans had to sit in a segregated area. In 1925 about 25,000 members of a racist organization, the Ku Klux Klan, marched down Pennsylvania Avenue. The event did not show the best side of the capital of a nation dedicated to freedom for all.

During the Great Depression of the 1930s, banks failed, businesses closed, and 13 million people were

The Jefferson Memorial can be seen through the cherry trees along the Tidal Basin.

out of work. Franklin D. Roosevelt was elected President to change that through strong federal programs. The government expanded enormously during this period—and so did the city's population.

In 1941 America entered World War II. As always, the national crisis made Washington, D.C., grow. It took three hundred people just to run the telephone switchboards in the new Pentagon building. Temporary buildings were put up all over the city, even along the Mall.

By the 1950s Washington, D.C., had a population of about eight hundred thousand people. The city had absorbed nearby communities such as George Town. The suburbs around the city were growing in both Maryland and Virginia.

The city's biggest challenge was civil rights. Decisions in the United States Supreme Court desegregated the city's schools, but the city itself was still segregated. In 1963 thousands of people came to Washington to demonstrate for civil rights. Dr. Martin Luther King, Jr., gave his "I Have a Dream" speech at that demonstration. The next year Congress passed the Civil Rights Act. This law desegregated all public places. Slowly, the changes were coming. Nonetheless, African Americans were increasingly frustrated. When Dr. Martin Luther King, Jr., was killed in 1968, Washington, D.C., had a week of protest riots that destroyed some neighborhoods.

The city's African American population climbed more than 71 percent during the 1970s. By 1990 African Americans made up about two thirds of the city's population. Despite laws against segregation, neighborhoods within the District of Columbia remained separate along color lines.

This mural by Don Miller can be seen at the Martin Luther King, Jr., Memorial Library. It depicts a voter registration drive during the civil rights movement.

The federal government has continued to grow, although the city's population has remained fairly stable. Many newcomers live in the suburbs that circle the city. By 1990 the District of Columbia had a population of 606,900, but the metropolitan area had 3,924,000 people.

Washington, D.C., is once again a city with some power over its own affairs. In 1961 the Constitution was amended so that citizens could vote in Presidential elections. In 1970 Congress allowed the District of Columbia to elect a delegate to the House, although this person couldn't vote on any issues. In 1973 people in the district were allowed to elect their own mayor and city council members. And in 1990 the city created a special office to be filled by two Statehood Senators, or "shadow senators." These people are working to get Congress to declare that the District of Columbia is a state, with full state's rights.

Many Washingtonians want the district to be a state, called New Columbia. Congress hasn't yet approved the idea. The citizens of the District of Columbia have had to fight for the right to govern themselves long after most Americans have taken that right for granted.

Eleanor Holmes Norton is the nonvoting delegate in Congress for Washington, D.C.

19

"The Soldier May Not Choose . . ."

"As I sit . . . I see a train of about thirty huge four-horse wagons, used as ambulances, filled with wounded . . . on their way, probably to Columbian, Carver, and Mount Pleasant hospitals. This is the way the men come . . . almost always in these long, sad processions." The date was 1863, about halfway through the Civil War.

The place was Washington, D.C., and the writer was Walt Whitman, a great American poet. He was one of the hundreds of people who worked as a hospital volunteer in the North or the South.

What was life like during the Civil War? During this time of history, there were no electric lights, paved roads, or sewer systems. There wasn't any clean running water, either. Garbage was piled in wide, open pits near the camps.

Wounded Union soldiers await transportation home after fighting the battle at Fredericksburg, Virginia, on May 3, 1863.

Medical care was very poor during the Civil War. There was no penicillin or any kind of antibiotic. At this time, people were just beginning to understand how a cut could get infected. No one knew how to sterilize medical instruments—or even that it should be done. Hard as it may be to believe, very few doctors had ever treated a gunshot wound. Unfortunately, this was the first war in the United States that was mostly fought with relatively modern weapons.

Matters were made worse due to overcrowding in the hospitals. Washington, D.C., had the responsibility of caring for thousands of sick and wounded soldiers. There were other people in the city besides soldiers needing medical care, too. There were more than 25 hospitals, but most of them had been something else before the fighting began. Sophronia Bucklin was a nurse in a "hospital" at the Judiciary Square Hotel. Her ward, or patients' room, was in the ballroom. She describes the scene this way: "I looked upon the narrow iron bedsteads furnished with one bed of straw, one straw pillow, two sheets, one blanket . . . , three

rows of which ran the length of the long room, forming narrow passage ways. . . ."

Walt Whitman also commented on the "hospitals." As a volunteer, he went from building to building, giving comfort and companionship to the wounded soldiers. He talked to them and helped them write letters home. Mr. Whitman supplied them with writing paper if they were able to write without his help. He brought with him fruit and nuts and other small gifts, which he distributed to the patients. Sometimes he gave out small amounts of money. One man used the money to buy milk when it was offered for sale in the ward.

Mr. Whitman said that it was strange to visit the wards that were set up in the Patent Office. This was formerly a business office that gave permits to inventors. "It was indeed a curious scene at night when lit up. The glass cases [which held models of inventions], the beds, the sick, the gallery above, and the marble pavement under foot. . . ."

Louisa May Alcott, an American writer best known for her novel *Little Women*, also served in the wards of

Walt Whitman was a journalist, an essayist, and a poet. He is best known for his book of poetry, Leaves of Grass.

Washington's hospitals. She wrote a series of essays she called "Hospital Sketches," describing her work and the soldiers that she met. On the very first day, she was mostly bothered by the dirt and the smell. When a new group of wounded soldiers was brought to the hospital, she made an effort to pull off a man's shoe. After some tugging, the soldier politely told her that she had a hold of his bare foot! It was so dirty that she didn't realize it. Louisa May Alcott worked as a nurse for six weeks until she became ill with typhoid fever, an infection of the lungs and intestines. The damage from the disease affected her health for the rest of her life.

The writers describe very plainly the soldiers' terrible wounds. When soldiers were shot in the arms or legs, doctors usually had to cut off the limb. They didn't have the knowledge or the medicines to do anything else. If the patient didn't get an infection, then he would recover.

Many patients did get a certain kind of infection called gangrene. In gangrene, the skin tissues get infected. The tissues then die, which causes more infection. The cycle keeps going until the patient dies. The statistics tell the story: about 360,000 Union soldiers died during the Civil War. Over half of those deaths were due to disease and infection. Confederate soldiers were not much better off.

About 164,000 died of disease. No one was spared; soldiers, nurses, and volunteers all were in danger.

Still, Walt Whitman, Sophronia Bucklin, and Louisa May Alcott were among the volunteers who didn't hesitate to help despite the dangers. As Ms. Bucklin said, "The soldier may not choose in what ditch he will die . . . and why was I better than our boys in blue?"

This photo of Louisa May Alcott was taken around 1860. She is best known for her novel Little Women, *but she also wrote several other books and worked in the woman suffrage and the temperance movements.*

Frederick Douglass: Freedom's Voice

The year is 1841, and a crowd has gathered for an antislavery rally in Nantucket, Massachusetts. A young African American is invited to speak. He is asked to describe his life as a slave. The young man has not prepared a speech, but he steps to the front of the crowd. He begins to speak in a voice both gentle and passionate. When he has finished, many in his audience are weeping.

Frederick Douglass was born into slavery in 1817. At the age of eight, he was sent to Baltimore to work as a servant. There his owner's wife secretly taught him to read. When Douglass's owner found out, he punished the boy. But that didn't stop Douglass from pursuing an education on his own. He knew that educating himself was the only way to survive.

When Frederick Douglass was sixteen, he was sent to work as a field hand. It was then that he learned the true meaning of slavery. He and the other slaves were forced to work long hours in the hot sun. Many died from exhaustion and disease. The plantation's manager was cruel, and he often beat the slaves.

In 1838 Frederick Douglass managed to escape to the North. He worked at a variety of jobs while avoiding the slave hunters who would return him to his owner.

On that day in 1841, when he was asked to speak at the rally, Frederick Douglass became a spokesperson for the antislavery movement.

Frederick Douglass was born Frederick Augustus Washington Bailey. He changed his name when he escaped from slavery, to keep slave hunters from finding him.

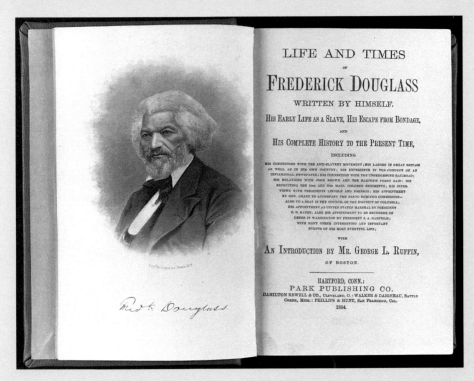

In 1855 Frederick Douglass wrote an expanded version of his famous autobiography and called it My Bondage and My Freedom. *In 1881 another version was published, this time under the title* Life and Times of Frederick Douglass.

He spoke so well, some people couldn't believe he had no formal education. Four years later he published an account of his life, *Narrative of the Life of Frederick Douglass, an American Slave.*

Frederick Douglass spent his later years in Washington, D.C. During the Civil War, President Abraham Lincoln made him an advisor. Douglass felt strongly that the war between the states was about one central issue— slavery. President Lincoln, in turn, rallied the North through speeches in which he insisted that slavery was wrong. Frederick Douglass also advised Lincoln that African Americans should be allowed to join the Union Army to fight. Lincoln took his advice.

After the war, Douglass held a number of governmental posts, including marshal and recorder of deeds. He served as the United States minister to Haiti from 1889 to 1891. Frederick Douglass kept fighting for human rights. On February 20, 1895, while attending a meeting on women's rights, Douglass collapsed. He died later the same day.

Frederick Douglass stands out as one of America's heroes in the fight for equal rights for all people.

Governing the Nation

What do you think most people in Washington, D.C., do for a living? Most people would say that in this particular city almost everyone works for the government. And that's partly right. When you add up all the different kinds of government jobs in Washington, D.C., the federal government employs over three hundred thousand people. However, elected officials make up just a small part of this group. Thousands of people work in government offices. There are typists, secretaries, and clerks. There are secret agents and limousine drivers. There are staff members, cooks, and people who park cars. If you think that there are a very large number of government workers, remember this. In 1980 the federal government employed four hundred thousand people! It may not seem like it, but the federal government is getting smaller, not larger.

Other people in the District of Columbia work in businesses that provide services. These service businesses include engineering companies, medical centers,

As in other major cities, rush hour in Washington, D.C., causes major traffic jams. Large numbers of people in the city drive cars to work.

This is the south lawn of the White House. From here you can look out at the Washington Monument, farther to the south. The President's helicopter often lands on the south lawn.

delivery trucks, and dry cleaners. Other service industries in our nation's capitol include telephone companies, newspapers, electricity and gas companies, and restaurants.

What else makes up the city's service industry? Thousands of people work as lobbyists, or representatives of special interest groups. There are lobbyists for farmers, doctors, telephone companies, oil companies, and environmental groups. In fact, about 2,500 associations and special interest groups have their headquarters in Washington, D.C. The city has a record number of lawyers, too. If you look at percentages, the population of Washington has a greater percentage of lawyers than any other state in the Union. When everything is added up, about three hundred thousand people work in the service industry.

Next to government and other services, the second most important part of Washington's economy is tourism. Every year, millions of people come to Washington because it is the nation's capital. Tourism brings in over $1.5 billion every year to the district and the surrounding areas.

It's easy to understand why Washington is so popular. Here people can experience the history of our country. They can see foreign embassies or attend festivals. They can visit the Capitol building and learn how our government works. All those things draw people from all over the country—indeed, from all over the world.

There isn't any agriculture in the District of Columbia. And there's very little manufacturing. Most manufacturing is printing and publishing. The Government Printing Office is the largest publishing "company" in the world. This office prints official

These people are lobbyists. They try to influence public officials and persuade legislators to either pass or vote against certain kinds of legislation.

Tourists are allowed to visit many rooms in the White House.

The Treasury Department's Bureau of Engraving and Printing prints seven thousand sheets of currency per hour.

transcripts of the proceedings of Congress. That means that if you want to read everything that goes on in the government—for instance, what goes on at a meeting of the Education Committee of the House of Representatives—you can purchase a copy from the Government Printing Office. This office also prints booklets to inform citizens about a huge number of topics. If you want to learn how to buy a new car, start a beekeeping business, make strawberry preserves, or use a parachute, the Government Printing Office has information you can use. It also prints a directory of all its publications.

The district is also home to private printing and publishing companies. The *Washington Post* hires more people than any other business employer in Washington. It is also one of the most influential newspapers in the country. Other companies produce special books and publications for groups such as the Smithsonian Institution, National Geographic, or any of the other associations and special interest groups in the city. Newspapers and magazines, such as *USA Today* and *U.S. News and World Report*, are also published in Washington.

The interest in publishing tells you that information is important to Washington's economy. That's true not only about printed materials but also about television, radio, and other media. The United States is a world power, so what happens in Washington, D.C., is important everywhere. People around the world want to know what's going on. The major television networks all have offices in the district. So do networks

These tourists are visiting the Lincoln Memorial, which contains a white marble statue of Abraham Lincoln. More than 52,000 people in Washington, D.C., have jobs in tourist-related industries.

The Library of Congress is the world's largest library. It contains over one hundred million publications. In an information-based economy, a library can be a critical resource.

such as C-SPAN. About 12,000 journalists and reporters work in the District of Columbia. And that isn't counting the journalists from other countries!

A large part of the economy of Washington, D.C., is connected to the federal government. People usually say that an economy that depends on just one industry can't be stable. If the industry has problems, people will lose their jobs and the economy of the area will be in trouble. Washington is safe from problems like this—unless the federal government shuts down. And no one thinks that's going to happen very soon.

Life in Congress

Washington, D.C., is a very impressive town. People feel awed, humbled, and amazed by it. After all, it's the capital of the United States— one of the most powerful countries in the world. It's a place where historic events happen and important laws are made. What's it like to be part of that?

Few people will ever know what it's like to be President of the United States. But many more people have discovered the feeling of being a member of Congress. The Senate and the House of Representatives are the two parts of Congress. Two senators are elected from every state. The

number of representatives from each state varies because each one represents a certain number of people. So states with lots of people have more representatives than states with few people.

Senators and representatives who are new to Washington can be just as amazed by the city as tourists are. "Oh, this is a heady town! You know that when I was sworn in to the Congress of the United States, I'd only been in the United States capital once?" That was Representative Stewart McKinney's reaction shortly after he came to Washington, D.C., in 1971 as a representative from Connecticut.

"I . . . voted against the President on the MX missile—and I was called down to the Oval Office for an 18-hour woodshed thing. And I had to sit there and say no to the President of the United States! That's heady stuff." That's one way Representative McKinney found out he really was in the city of power.

Another way was having lobbyists give him special attention. Lobbyists want to influence government decisions. They are called lobbyists because they often meet legislators in the lobby outside the meeting rooms of Congress. There the lobbyists try to persuade members of Congress to pass laws that favor the lobbyists' interests.

That's an example of what life in Congress is like. But there's a personal side, too. Many representatives and senators in Washington, D.C., are far from home. Often their families move to the Washington area while they're in office. Others stay in their home state. Either way the job requires a lot of traveling to and from the nation's capital. Representatives must also find time to keep in touch with the people who elected them. Their work requires long hours. But most think it's worth it. After all, they are helping make the country work!

United States Representatives have been meeting in these chambers for almost two hundred years.

Our Nation's Treasure

When people make statements about the culture of Washington, D.C., they usually mean the culture of the United States. That is because Washington, D.C., is home to many of our national treasures. One of these is the Smithsonian Institution. The Smithsonian is the largest museum complex in the world. It has more than one hundred million specimens and artifacts.

The Smithsonian Institution began as a gift from an Englishman named James Smithson. In his will he gave half a million dollars to the United States. The money was to be spent on an institution to increase and spread knowledge. The Smithsonian was created by Congress in 1846.

Today, the Smithsonian has 14 museums and galleries, plus research facilities outside the district. In the Smithsonian's National Portrait Gallery you can see paintings of people who have been important in the United States. For example, there are portraits of Presidents, sports figures, movie stars, writers, and composers. The Freer Gallery of Art displays art from

The Smithsonian Castle, built in the 1840s, was the Smithsonian Institution's first home.

American artists of the nineteenth and twentieth centuries.

The National Air and Space Museum is the most visited museum in the world. This collection traces the history of flight from the earliest airplanes to space travel. Visitors can get a close look at everything from the Wright Brothers' 1903 flyer to the *Apollo 11* lunar command module. This huge building also houses the *Spirit of St. Louis*, World War II airplanes, moon rocks, and other treasures.

The National Museum of American History deals with everyday life in the American past. It includes exhibits of items that date back as far as the Revolutionary War. Among the most popular displays are the original flag that inspired the "Star Spangled Banner" and a collection of gowns worn by Presidents' wives. Another favorite display is that of the ruby slippers worn by young Judy Garland, who played "Dorothy" in the movie *The Wizard of Oz*.

Some of the museums and galleries feature works from other parts of the world. For instance, the Arthur M. Sackler Gallery features paintings and other art from Southeast Asia. The Smithsonian's National Museum of African Art is the home of more than six thousand items such as tribal masks, sculptures, and textiles from all over Africa. The Smithsonian Institution also has much much more. That must be why American author Mark Twain called the Smithsonian "the nation's attic."

Washington, D.C., has other important museums, as well. The Corcoran Gallery of Art is the oldest

This figure on a horse stands in the National Museum of African Art. It is a hard clay sculpture from the inland delta region of Mali.

The East Building of the National Gallery of Art, which opened in 1978, is devoted to contemporary artists.

The Statuary Hall in the Capitol contains statues of legendary people from each state. This statue depicts Father Damien, a Catholic missionary who tended people who were sick with leprosy on the island of Molokai, Hawaii.

gallery in the city and one of the three oldest galleries in the nation not supported by government funds. It is also considered one of the best galleries in the country.

Sculpture is an art form that is widely displayed throughout Washington, D.C. Statuary Hall is in the Capitol. The statues in this building represent honored Americans from a number of states. For instance, Hawaii sent a statue of Father Damien, a Catholic priest who worked in a leper colony on the Hawaiian island of Molokai. The display includes people who wrote the Declaration of Independence and fought in the Revolutionary War. You'll also see a beloved humorist, the inventor of an alphabet for the Cherokee, and the first female to belong to the National Academy of Science.

Some of the most marvelous examples of sculpture are the statues and monuments that are outdoors. Many of these monuments are familiar, like the Marine

Corps War Memorial, the Lincoln Memorial, the Washington Monument, and the Jefferson Memorial. Visitors consider the Vietnam War Memorial, also called "The Wall," a special place. Carved into the black granite of the wall are the names of all those who died in that war. Visitors often make copies of the names and leave gifts on the ground in memory of those who died. Sculptures there honor all the men and women who fought in the Vietnam War.

Music, ballet, and drama are all part of what are called the performing arts. The best-known place in Washington, D.C., to view these arts is probably the John F. Kennedy Center for the Performing Arts. You'll find the National Symphony Orchestra, the Washington Opera, and the American Film Institute at the Kennedy Center. Special events at the Kennedy Center are often televised so that all Americans can see one of their national treasures at its best.

Washington, D.C., is a city of parks. The National Zoological Park has more than five thousand animals. The National Zoo, which is part of Rock Creek Park,

covers two hundred acres of land. It was created in 1890 to preserve the natural landscape of the Potomac River basin. The Kenilworth Aquatic Gardens lies along the Anacostia River. It was founded by W. B. Shaw at the end of the nineteenth century. The Aquatic Gardens features many types of flowers, plants, and animals that live and grow in water. Since it was founded, the Aquatic Gardens has become a highly valued wetland.

The New York City Ballet is shown here performing at the John F. Kennedy Center for the Performing Arts.

Washington, D.C., is also home to the largest library in the world, the Library of Congress. The library contains more than one hundred million items. Tours are allowed in many buildings of the federal government. These include the FBI building, the Capitol building, the National Archives, and even the White House!

This giant panda at the National Zoo was a gift from China. The National Zoo is home to many rare and protected animals.

The Vietnam War Memorial is inscribed with the names of each of the 58,219 Americans who were killed or reported missing in the Vietnam War. The memorial, a black granite, V-shaped wall, was designed by Maya Ying Lin.

A Cathedral for the Nation

The architect Pierre L'Enfant had many plans for Washington, D.C. One thing that he wanted was a national cathedral. L'Enfant explained that he did not want the cathedral to be associated with any particular religion, but, rather, equally open to all. In 1907 L'Enfant's plan was realized, and President Theodore Roosevelt laid the foundation stone, the very first stone. Eighty-three years later, in 1990, the project was completed. It is the sixth largest cathedral in the world.

The National Cathedral is perched on a hill called Mount St. Albans. It is built of blocks of limestone, each weighing about three hundred pounds. The cathedral was built in the Gothic style. This style refers to a type of architecture that was typical in Europe from the twelfth to the sixteenth centuries. In an effort to keep to this style, the cathedral was built without any modern materials or supports. The entire structure is made of stone. Looking straight up in the main section of the cathedral, one can see the high arches of the ceiling, 102 feet above the floor. Two hundred stained glass windows, also common

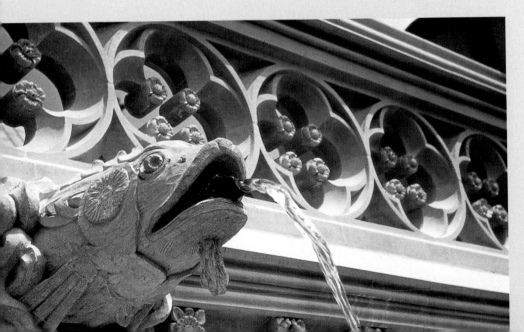

Water spouts out of the mouth of this gargoyle on the National Cathedral.

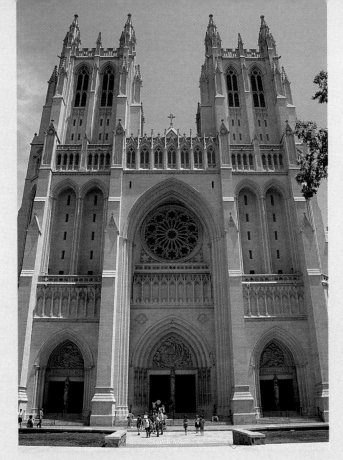

Dr. Martin Luther King, Jr., preached his last Sunday sermon at the National Cathedral.

in Gothic architecture, adorn the walls.

Many skilled stone workers contributed their talents in building this cathedral. There are more than three thousand special hand-made carvings in the cathedral. The stone workers were often allowed to choose their own designs. Among these are rosettes, Native American kachinas, totems, and even the faces of a cat and a dog. The carvings were placed wherever workers felt the cathedral needed a decorative touch.

Maybe the most interesting stone carvings are the gargoyles that decorate the outside of the building. A gargoyle is a carved form of a human or an animal figure. Sometimes they are monstrous-looking creatures. Gargoyles are carved so that water can run through an opening, usually a mouth. Their practical purpose is to drain water off the roof, just like gutters and downspouts on a house. Gargoyles are common decorations on Gothic architecture. While the cathedral was being built, thousands of Americans suggested modern topics for the gargoyles. Today, there are over one hundred gargoyles on the cathedral, and no two are alike.

The National Cathedral is an Episcopal church, but it is national in scope and traditional in design.

The State of the Future

There are two ways to look at Washington, D.C. First of all, the district is a place where people live and work, just as they do anywhere else in the United States. The district is also the center of our federal government.

Many of the people who live in Washington, D.C., are in favor of making the district a state. Statehood would give the residents of the district a voice in the federal government, which they do not have at the present time. A majority of the district's citizens want to send people to Congress who will represent their views on national issues.

People who are against the idea talk about the tiny size of the district. Would it matter that the new state is so small? New Columbia, as the new state would be called, would be smaller than most counties. In fact, it would be smaller than most large cities! But very large states and very small states are nothing new in the United States. Look at a map. How many times would states the size of Delaware or Rhode Island fit inside

Remembering the past helps people move into the future. Every year on the Fourth of July, fireworks commemorate the signing of the Declaration of Independence.

either Alaska or Texas? That's why our Constitution specifies that there should be two parts to Congress. Every state has two senators, no matter how big or small the state is. Every state also selects members of the House of Representatives according to the number of people who live in the state. The number of representatives in the House is fixed at 435. Every ten years that number is divided among the states according to population.

Whether or not it becomes a state, Washington, D.C., has serious problems to deal with in the coming years. As in other large cities, many people have moved to the outer communities, or suburbs. This is a big problem because cities use taxes collected from its residents to pay for public services, such as public schools and fire and police forces. As a result, it has become harder and harder for the city to meet the basic needs of its citizens. Also, the law states that federal buildings can't be taxed—and half of all the buildings in Washington, D.C., are federal buildings. So, the city has to look beyond property taxes for creative solutions.

The District of Columbia is more than just a city, however. It is also the seat of our federal government. Washington's future is tied to America's future. No one knows what will happen in the years to come. So the future of Washington, D.C., will be very challenging—and difficult to predict.

Abraham Lincoln grew from humble beginnings to lead the nation through one of the most difficult times in its history. He remains a worthy role model to follow as our nation enters the twenty-first century.

44

Important Historical Events

1608 John Smith explores the area near the Potomac River that later becomes Washington, D.C.

1790 A compromise between northern and southern states is made, and a southern location is agreed on for the nation's capital.

1791 A site along the Potomac River is chosen for the nation's capital. President George Washington appoints Pierre Charles L'Enfant to design the city.

1792 L'Enfant is fired. Andrew Ellicott and his assistant, Benjamin Banneker, take over the job.

1800 Washington, D.C., officially becomes the nation's capital.

1814 The British burn buildings in Washington, D.C., during the War of 1812.

1829 Congress receives a bequest from James Smithson. The money is to be used to found an institution to promote knowledge.

1846 The government returns Alexandria to Virginia.

1861 to 1865 Union soldiers fortify Washington, D.C., to protect it from the Confederacy during the Civil War.

1871 Washington, D.C., becomes a federal territory.

1874 Congress creates a local government made up of commissioners appointed by the President. Washington, D.C., is the only American city that does not elect its own officials.

1885 The Washington Monument is dedicated.

1917 The United States enters World War I. There is another large population growth in Washington, D.C.

1922 The Lincoln Memorial is completed.

1941 The United States enters World War II. Once again the population grows rapidly.

1944 Representatives of the United States, Great Britain, the Soviet Union, and China meet at a park called Dumbarton Oaks to design the organization known as the United Nations.

1950 Washington's population growth peaks at eight hundred thousand.

1961 District residents are given the right to vote in presidential elections.

1963 At a Civil Rights demonstration, Dr. Martin Luther King, Jr., delivers his "I Have a Dream" speech from the steps of the Lincoln Memorial.

1968 Riots break out in the city when Dr. Martin Luther King, Jr., is assassinated.

1970 Washington elects its first nonvoting delegate to the House of Representatives.

1973 Residents are given the right to elect their own local government officials.

1980 The majority of Washington voters support a proposal for statehood.

1982 A constitutional convention is held, and a constitution is written for New Columbia.

1993 President Bill Clinton and other world leaders dedicate the United States Holocaust Memorial Museum.

The district's flag shows two red bars and three stars on a field of white. The design is based on George Washington's coat of arms, or family emblem.

Washington, D.C., Almanac

District Bird. Wood thrush

District Flower. American beauty rose

District Tree. Scarlet oak

District Motto. *Justitia Omnibus* (Justice for All)

District Abbreviations. D.C. (traditional); DC (postal)

Founded. Site chosen, 1791. Became nation's capital, 1800

Government. Washington, D.C., is a federal district and is not a part of any state. Washington, D.C., is under the authority of Congress. Residents, however, elect their own mayor and a 13-person council. The district has one nonvoting delegate to the House of Representatives.

Area. 68 sq mi (176 sq km)

Greatest Distances. north/south, approximately 14 mi (23 km); east/west, approximately 9 mi (15 km)

Elevation. 25 ft (7.6 m) above sea level

Population. 1990 Census: 606,900 (5.6% decrease from 1980). Density: 8,925 persons per sq mi (3,448 persons per sq km). 1980 Census: 638,333

Economy. Federal government. *Manufacturing:* printing and publishing

District Bird: Wood thrush

District Flower:
American beauty rose

Annual Events

★ Chinese New Year Parade (February)

★ Smithsonian Kite Festival (March)

★ Easter Egg Roll on White House lawn (April)

★ National Cherry Blossom Festival (April)

★ Festival of American Folklife (June–July)

★ Independence Day Celebration (July 4)

★ Shakespeare Festival (August)

★ Washington International Horse Show (October)

★ Lighting of the National Christmas Tree (December)

Places to Visit

★ Capital Children's Museum

★ John F. Kennedy Center for the Performing Arts

★ Martin Luther King, Jr., Memorial Library

★ National Museum of African Art

★ National Air and Space Museum

★ National Museum of American History

★ National Zoological Park

★ Smithsonian Institution

★ United States Holocaust Memorial Museum

★ Washington Monument

★ White House

District Seal